Novel Know How

Novel activities for any fictional text

Book 1

Janet Bruce

essential
resources

Title:	Novel Know How Novel activities for any fictional text: Book 1
Author:	Janet Bruce
Editor:	Paula Wagemaker
Layout:	Freshfields Design Limited
Book code:	5421
ISBN:	978-1-877478-73-4
Published:	2009
Publisher:	Essential Resources Educational Publishers Limited

United Kingdom:	*Australia:*	*New Zealand:*
Unit 8–10 Parkside	PO Box 90	PO Box 5036
Shortgate Lane	Oak Flats	Invercargill 9810
Laughton	NSW 2529	
BN8 6DG	ph: 1800 005 068	ph: 0800 087 376
ph: 0845 3636 147	fax: 1800 981 213	fax: 0800 937 825
fax: 0845 3636 148		

Websites: essentialresourcesuk.com
www.essentialresources.com.au
www.essentialresources.co.nz

About the author: Janet Bruce has taught at all levels of the primary school in Australia. As a curriculum coordinator, her primary responsibilities were to develop the school-based English curriculum. This series has emerged from her passion for reading and inspiring children to develop a love of reading. The open-ended tasks that appear in this fun resource are a product of her detailed knowledge of English and literacy curricula, as well as her varied classroom experience.

Contents

Introduction

This *Novel Know How* series contains a range of open-ended, engaging activities that are suitable to use with any fictional novel being studied in the secondary English classroom.

The Task Cards

The activities are presented in the form of task cards. You can use them for whole class activities, individual activities or partner-based work. The task cards offer a range of fun, varied, stimulating activities that increase students' comprehension of and engagement with the novel they are reading.

The task cards offer a broad range of engaging activities in the following areas.

 ## Comprehension and Detail

The aim of these activities is to develop students' comprehension. The activities are varied and encourage the students to engage with the text to extract greater meaning.

 ## Language and Vocabulary

These activities focus on language, grammar, understanding, and applying new vocabulary. They encourage students to seek out, identify, understand and apply new and interesting words.

 ## Artist and Illustrator

These activities explore the creative and visual aspects of the novel. They explore the emotions and pictures created in our minds when we hear particular words, phrases and passages. In completing the activities, students visualise their thoughts and feelings in relation to the text and re-create them artistically.

 ## Reflecting and Responding

These activities ask students to reflect on and respond to a particular aspect of their text as a way of provoking a written response. Students are particularly interested in these activities because they can respond in a personal manner.

UK Curriculum Links

Key Stage 2 (Year 6 progression to Year 7)

Learning strand	Objective(s) *Most children learn to:*
7. Understanding and interpreting texts	• read between the lines and find evidence for their interpretation • Infer the meanings of unknown words using syntax, context, word structures and origins
8. Engaging with and responding to texts	• write reflectively about a text, distinguishing between the attitudes and assumptions of characters and those of the author and taking account of the needs of others who might read it
9. Creating and shaping texts	• independently write and present a text with the reader and purpose in mind • experiment with the visual and sound effects of language, including the use of imagery, alliteration, rhythm and rhyme.

Source: Adapted from the Primary Framework for Literacy and Maths 2006

Key Stage 3 (Years 7–8)

Areas of learning	Objectives
Reading – 5 Reading for meaning: understanding and responding to print, electronic and multi-modal texts	
5.1 Developing and adapting active reading skills and strategies	• Extract the main points and relevant information from a text or source using a range of strategies such as skimming and scanning. • Use inference and deduction to recognise implicit meanings at sentence and text level. • Use a range of reading strategies to retrieve relevant information and main points from texts, distinguishing between fact and opinion where appropriate. • Use inference and deduction to explore layers of meaning within a text. • Make relevant notes when gathering ideas from texts. • Make relevant notes when researching different sources, comparing and contrasting information.
5.2 Understanding and responding to ideas, viewpoints, themes and purposes in texts	• Identify and understand the main ideas, viewpoints, themes and purposes in a text. • Make a personal response to a text and provide some textual reference in support. • Trace the development of a writer's ideas, viewpoint and themes. • Respond to a text by making precise points and providing relevant evidence in support of those points.
5.3 Reading and engaging with a wide and varied range of texts	• Make informed personal choices of texts and express their preferences. • Understand how readers choose and respond to texts. • Broaden their experience of reading a wide range of texts and express their preferences and opinions. • Explore how different audiences choose and respond to texts.
Reading – 6 Understanding the author's craft	
6.2 Analysing how writers' use of linguistic and literary features shapes and influences meaning	• Identify and describe the effect of writers' use of specific literary, rhetorical and grammatical features. • Explore the range, variety and overall effect on readers of literary, rhetorical and grammatical features used by writers of literary and non-literary texts.

Source: Adapted from the Framework for Secondary English 2008

Australian Curriculum Links

State/territory	Source	Strands	Objectives
ACT	Curriculum Framework for ACT Schools Preschool to Year 10	Essential Learning Areas	1. The student uses a range of strategies to think and learn. 2. The student understands and applies the inquiry process. 3. The student makes considered decisions. 9. The student reads effectively. 10. The student writes effectively. 11. The student critically interprets and creates texts.
NSW	English 7–10 Syllabus Stage 4	Reading Writing	Through responding to and composing a wide range of texts in context and through close study of texts, students will develop skills, knowledge and understanding in order to: • speak, listen, read, write, view and represent • use language and communicate appropriately and effectively • think in ways that are imaginative, interpretive and critical • express themselves and their relationships with others and the world • learn and reflect on their learning through their study of English.
NT	NT Curriculum Framework English Learning Area – Band 4	Reading and viewing Writing	**R/V 4.1 Texts and contexts:** construct interpretive responses demonstrating knowledge that texts are created for a particular audience and purpose; develop intertextual understanding. **R/V 4.2 Language structures and features:** describe techniques used to shape audience response to literary, film, media and everyday texts. **R/V 4.3 Strategies:** use strategies to identify and respond to the way conventions shape meaning in a range of texts. **W 4.1 Texts and contexts:** plan, compose and edit a range of sustained and developed texts appropriate to audience, purpose and context. **W 4.2 Language structures and features:** control language structures and features necessary to communicate ideas and information clearly in written texts of some length and complexity. **W 4.3 Strategies:** use a range of strategies to plan, compose, review and edit written texts for meaning and effectiveness.
QLD	English Year 7 Essential Learnings	Reading and viewing Writing and designing Language elements	Reading and viewing involve using a range of strategies to interpret, evaluate and appreciate written, visual and multimodal texts across wider community contexts. Writing and designing involve using language elements to construct literary and non-literary texts for audiences across wider community contexts. Interpreting and constructing texts involve selecting and controlling choices about grammar, punctuation, vocabulary, audio and visual elements, in print-based, electronic and face-to-face modes (speaking and listening, reading and viewing, writing and designing) across wider community contexts.

Australian Curriculum Links (continued)

State/ territory	Source	Strands	Objectives
SA	Curriculum Standards and Accountability Framework Middle Years band	Texts and contexts	As students read and view texts they learn to: • engage with a range of written and visual texts for different purposes interpret and respond to different texts [KC1] [KC2] • demonstrate critical understanding of texts [KC1] • use information and communication technologies and critically analyse electronic information for accuracy and quality [KC7].
VIC	Victorian Essential Learning Standards, English Level 4	Reading	**Reading** At Level 4, students read, interpret and respond to a wide range of literary, everyday and media texts in print and in multimodal formats. They analyse these texts and support interpretations with evidence drawn from the text. They describe how texts are constructed for particular purposes, and identify how sociocultural values, attitudes and beliefs are presented in texts. They analyse imagery, characterisation, dialogue, point of view, plot and setting. They use strategies such as reading on, using contextual cues, and drawing on knowledge of text organisation when interpreting texts containing unfamiliar ideas and information.
		Writing	**Writing** At Level 4, students produce, in print and electronic forms, a variety of texts for different purposes using structures and features of language appropriate to the purpose, audience and context of the writing. They begin to use simple figurative language and visual images. They use a range of vocabulary and a variety of sentence structures, and use punctuation accurately, including apostrophes. They identify and use different parts of speech, including nouns, pronouns, adverbs, comparative adverbs and adjectives, and use appropriate prepositions and conjunctions. They use a range of approaches to spelling, applying morphemic knowledge and an understanding of visual and phonic patterns. They employ a variety of strategies for writing, including note-making, using models, planning, editing and proofreading.
TAS	K–10 Syllabus English Literacy Standard 3	Reading and viewing	Reading and viewing a range of texts.
		Writing and representing	Writing and representing for a range of purposes and audiences.
		Thinking	Thinking logically, critically, creatively and reflectively.
WA	English Learning Area Statement	Viewing	**Viewing 7.** Students view a wide range of visual texts with purpose, understanding and critical awareness.
		Reading	**Reading 8.** Students read a wide range of texts with purpose, understanding and critical awareness.
		Writing	**Writing 9.** Students write for a range of purposes and in a range of forms using conventions appropriate to audience, purpose and context.

New Zealand Curriculum Links

Level 3: Making meaning and creating meaning

Learning strand	Objective(s) *Students will:*
Processes and strategies	• integrate sources of information, processes and strategies with developing confidence to identify, form and express ideas
Purposes and audiences	• show a developing understanding of how texts are shaped for different purposes and audiences
Ideas	• show a developing understanding of ideas within, across and beyond texts
Language features	• show a developing understanding of how language features are used for effect within and across texts
Structure	• show a developing understanding of text structures.

Level 4: Making meaning and creating meaning

Learning strand	Objective(s) *Students will:*
Processes and strategies	• integrate sources of information, processes and strategies confidently to identify, form and express ideas
Purposes and audiences	• show an increasing understanding of how texts are shaped for different purposes and audiences
Ideas	• show an increasing understanding of ideas within, across and beyond texts
Language features	• show an increasing understanding of how language features are used for effect within and across texts
Structure	• show an increasing understanding of text structures.

Source: Online version of English in the New Zealand Curriculum

Comprehension and Detail

Aim

The aim of the comprehension and detail activities is to develop students' comprehension and understanding of the text. The activities encourage students to engage with the text to extract a greater depth of meaning and understanding.

Comprehension and Detail

CARD 1

Memory Master

Write a detailed summary to describe the main events that occurred in the section of the novel you have just read. Your summary should include specific details and significant events.

Comprehension and Detail

CARD 2

Quizzical Questions

Create a bank of unusual, baffling or comical questions about the actual events and characters in the novel you are reading. Be sure to write the answers to your questions as well.

- Write THREE *unusual* questions.
- Write THREE *baffling* questions.
- Write THREE *comical* questions.

Test your questions on another person in your group.

CARD 3

Main Idea Melting Pot

The main ideas in the novel are the key events that are important to the development of the storyline. In your exercise novel, draw a picture of a big melting pot. Inside the pot, write all of the ingredients or main events the author wrote about to develop the story. The main ideas placed in your pot should include the most significant events that took place.

CARD 4

Colourful Character Feelings

Choose ONE character from your novel and record the different emotions and feelings this character experienced during different stages of the story. Be sure to state the reasons why the character was experiencing these emotions.

CARD 5

Acceptable Title

Study the title given to the novel you are reading. Do you think the author chose an appropriate title for the storyline depicted in this novel? Discuss the title given and outline your reasons for supporting or opposing the choice of title for this novel.

CARD 6

Cool Character

Choose a terrific character from your novel who did something exciting or memorable. Write an article for a children's magazine that tells students of your age all about this cool character. Remember to:

- Come up with a good title.

- Introduce and describe your character.

- Describe the exciting or memorable event in detail.

- Finish your article with a statement about why your character is cool so as to create a satisfying ending.

- Draw a picture of your character to accompany the magazine article.

CARD 7

Character Comparison

Compare and contrast the main character with another character in the novel. Your comparison must include information about the characters' personalities, actions, thoughts, words and motivations.

You will need to include specific details from the text in your response. A Venn diagram will help you organise your thoughts about the characters' similarities and differences.

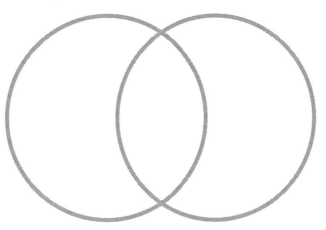

Venn diagram

CARD 8

Reading Actions

Authors often let the reader know exactly how their characters are feeling by having them act in a certain way in the story. Locate a section in the story where you knew exactly how a character felt because of his or her actions. Maybe this character was happy, excited, brave, selfish, funny, evil, worried or disappointed. Write this passage down in your exercise book and explain what it was about the writing that helped you understand how the character felt or acted, even though the author did not explicitly state that the character was sad, happy or whatever.

Two Minutes

Prepare a two-minute talk about your novel that you can present to your class. Be sure to provide information about the characters, the storyline and the parts you enjoyed the most. At the end of your talk, be ready to answer questions from your teacher and the class.

Interesting Interview

Prepare an interview with a partner. One of you takes the role of the author, and the other takes the role of the reporter. The reporter asks the author a series of questions about the novel. The author responds with information about the novel.

Literary Links

Write a report on the novel you are reading. Briefly outline the characters and describe the storyline. Comment on the use of imagery, symbolism and figurative language. Provide examples from the text to support your comments.

Sensible Scanning

Each member of the group opens their novel to the same page. The task for each of you is to scan the page to find as many *adjectives* as you can. An adjective is a descriptive word. Write down each adjective as you find it and tally the number you have found when the time is up. You have five minutes to find the adjectives. Share your list with the group and check the page in the novel to see if, as a group, you have collected them all.

Story Sequel

Now that you have finished the novel, think about how this story might continue. How could the story develop further to create a second novel?

Brainstorm your ideas for a second novel and discuss these with your group.

Story Pyramid

Create a story pyramid by following the directions below. Your story information should look like a pyramid when complete.

Line 1:   Write the name of the novel.

Line 2:   Write the name of the main character.

Line 3:   Write the names of two other characters.

Line 4:   Write four words to describe the setting.

Line 5:   Write six words to describe the main event.

Line 6:   Write nine words to describe the ending.

Powerful Passages

Powerful passages are phrases or sentences that leave an impression on the reader. Sometimes they leave an impression because the writing paints a vivid picture in the mind. Other times it might be because the writing changes the way the reader thinks about something or someone. Choose THREE powerful passages from your novel and explain why you found them powerful.

Cryptic Quiz

Create a cryptic quiz that really makes the other members of your group think about each of your questions. Each question should be tricky and require good knowledge of the details in the novel. Cryptic questions usually combine two or more questions at once, which means that anyone trying to answer each cryptic question will need to know the answer to each of its "sub-questions".

Do You Know?

A tourist has asked you for directions from one place in your novel to another. Write the directions down for this person so he or she can safely get to the desired location.

Sequencing Events

Create a list of TEN of the most significant events that took place in your novel. Write each event on a small piece of paper and alongside the name of the event draw a matching picture. Be sure not to number the events. Give the cards to another person in your group. Ask this person to sequence the events in the order in which they occurred.

Mum, Dad, George and maddie went to Ireland to catch fish. Dad fell ill, everyone was hungry.

Maddie took the boat to catch fish. The boat sank. George went to help.

George rescued Maddie and rowed her to safety. mum and Dad thanked George.

From the Perspective of . . .

Rewrite a summary of the novel from a different perspective. For example, you might choose to take the point of view of a cat, a hat, a shoe, a bird or a bag. When you have decided what perspective to adopt, think carefully about how the story will need to change so that it can be written from this new angle.

Sounds Like This

Foley artists add sounds to movies, to enhance the actions. They have to think of the smallest sounds to include in the final recording. For example, if someone kicks a bottle along the road, the Foley artist needs to insert the pinging sound of the bottle when it is kicked, the rolling of the bottle along the ground, and the steps of the person walking along. Read a section of your novel and write down all of the sounds described in that section.

CARD 21

Beautiful Blurb

Read the blurb on the back of the novel. Write down at least one positive and one negative point about the blurb. Think about the points you have noted and rewrite the blurb to improve the current information given to prospective readers.

CARD 22

True or False?

Write down a mixture of at least ten true and false statements about events that took place in the novel you are reading. Read these statements to another person who has read the novel and test their knowledge.

Language and Vocabulary

Aim

These activities focus on the language, grammar and vocabulary within the text. The activities encourage students to seek out, identify, understand and apply new and interesting words.

Brilliant Bookmark

Create a brilliant bookmark to record any fresh and fascinating words you come across as you read your novel. The words you write on your bookmark should be a mixture of new words you have not seen before and evocative words you might like to remember to use in your own writing.

Interesting Imagery

Choose a chapter in your novel and study the descriptive passages in this section. Make a list of the vivid similes, metaphors, alliteration, noun phrases and other figures of speech that help to create images in your mind.

Dictionary Database

A dictionary contains all of the words of a language written in alphabetical order. Dictionaries are useful because they allow you to find the meaning and pronunciation of a word. As you read your novel, write down interesting and unusual words. Use these words to create your own dictionary, which you can then use as a database of words for use in your own writing. Set out your page in the following way:

Novel Dictionary

Quixotic: unrealistic and impractical

Tranquil: calm and undisturbed

Time Adverbs

Adverbs are words that provide the reader with more information about the verb (action). *Manner adverbs* are used to show *how* something happened. Some examples are rapidly, slowly, fast, limping. Read a section of your novel and list as many different manner adverbs as you can find. Write these in your exercise novel. Use this list to assist you when you are writing.

Mood and Atmosphere

Authors create mood and atmosphere by using clever language choices. Describe the mood the author sets in the novel you are reading (for example, spooky, creepy, sweet, funny, exciting). Explain in your own words how the author created this feeling.

Splendid Satire

Satire is the use of sharp wit or humour to highlight stupidities that have occurred. The aim is to entertain the reader through humour. Satire creates funny moments based around silly actions. Find as many examples of the use of satire from your novel as you can and write them down.

Hysterical Hyperbole

Hyperbole is a figure of speech that uses over-exaggeration. What is said is not meant to be taken literally. Hyperbole also uses humour to emphasise a point. Here are two examples of hyperbole: "I told you a billion times not to exaggerate" and "We had enough food to feed an army." Look through your novel and locate as many examples of hyperbole as you can find. Write these down as a list.

Situational Irony

Situational irony is when the opposite of what is expected to happen takes place. Describe ONE event from your novel where the opposite of what you expected took place. Describe your thoughts about what you expected to happen.

Elated Euphemism

Euphemisms express an unpleasant or uncomfortable situation in a more sensitive and kind manner. The purpose of euphemisms is to soften the blow and protect people's feelings. An example is "Your dog passed away" instead of "Your dog is dead." Write down some examples of euphemisms from your novel.

Critical Climax

A *climax* is a build-up of ideas. The climax occurs when these ideas reach a critical peak. The climax is created by building up interest and excitement for the reader. Locate ONE climax from your novel. Write down the section from the novel and describe the event in your own words.

Symbolic Expressions

Authors use *symbolic expressions* to exaggerate or compare situations or characters. The author aims to express a meaning that is different from the one given. Here are some examples:

- Clare broke the ice [that is, she was the first to speak].

- The student was on edge [he was nervous].

- Billy got out of bed on the wrong side [he was grumpy—in a bad mood].

Find as many examples of symbolic expressions from your novel as you can. Write the meaning next to each expression.

Colloquial Language

Colloquial language is informal, casual, conversational, everyday speech. In written form, colloquial language makes what is said sound natural and convincing. If the author was writing a conversation between two teenagers, we would expect to see colloquial language.

Example:

"What's your *old man* up to?"

"He's having a *chinwag* with the *postie*."

Write the names of each character in your novel. List examples of colloquial language used by each character.

Jargon

Jargon is the collection of words, phrases and expressions used exclusively by different groups of people. This "inside" language expresses ideas frequently used by a particular group, such as businesspeople. Look through your novel and identify uses of jargon by the characters in your novel. Write the name of each character and the jargon he or she uses throughout the novel.

Subjectivity/Objectivity

- *Subjectivity* refers to unfair and one-sided points of view. Subjective statements are biased statements that favour a particular point of view.

- *Objectivity* involves taking a fair point of view and considering all sides of an argument or debate. Objective statements are unbiased statements that look beyond just one point of view.

Find examples of subjective and objective statements from your novel. Be sure to write down who said each statement.

Other Oxymorons

An *oxymoron* places two contradictory words next to each other. These words create a powerful image in the reader's mind. Examples of oxymoron include the following: pretty ugly; long shorts; all alone; awfully good; bittersweet; doing nothing; big baby. Read through a section of your novel and write as many examples of oxymoron as you can find.

Sensationalism

Sensationalism is the deliberate use of dramatic words. These words are used to excite, horrify or provoke interest in the reader. By over-dramatising a situation, this technique creates a great deal of interest and attention. Locate one section of your novel where the author sensationalises a particular event. List the type of language the author uses to enthuse and excite the reader.

Vibrant Vowels

Choose a few sentences from the novel. Write these sentences in your exercise novel, but leave out all the vowels. Here is an example:

Without the vowels: Th qck brwn fx jmpd vr th lzy dg.

With the vowels: The quick brown fox jumped over the lazy dog.

Swap your sentences with another person and get your partner to write the next few sentences from the novel, but also without the vowels. Check each other's sentences when finished.

Secret Message

Write a secret message to your friend telling him or her about a surprise or shock moment in your novel. Write your message in code so that other people cannot read the message. Write your message using the letter that comes after the correct letter in the alphabet.

a	b	c	d	e	f	g	h	i	j	k	l	m	n	o	p	q	r	s	t	u	v	w	x	y	z
b	c	d	e	f	g	h	i	j	k	l	m	n	o	p	q	r	s	t	u	v	w	x	y	z	a

Shape Words

Draw a tree, but only the trunk and the branches. Choose a range of words from your novel that have a shape. Write the words in shapes to form the leaves of the tree and glue them onto the branches. For example, with the word *fire*, write "fire" to fit within a flame-shaped leaf. With the word *water*, write "water" to fit within a leaf that is the shape of a water drop.

Jumbled Words

Choose TEN words from your novel to create jumbled word problems for other group members to solve.

Examples:

LLAUBRME: We use this to to protect us from the rain and from sunshine.

EKINF: We use this to cut food.

Wicked Wordsmith

In the novel you are reading, locate a well-written passage that demonstrates excellent use of descriptive words. Record this passage in your novel. Then write a commentary on this piece of writing, outlining your opinions about the effectiveness of its descriptive elements.

Character Crossword

Make a list of words that are connected to a particular character in the novel you are reading. Use these words as the basis for creating a crossword. When your crossword is complete, swap it with someone else's.

Artist and Illustrator

Aim

These activities explore creativity and visualisation. They investigate the emotions and images that are created in our minds when we hear particular words, phrases and passages. The activities enable students to visualise the thoughts and feelings they have in relation to the text and to re-create these visually.

Word Art Calligrams

Calligrams are designs that use the letters of their word. Words can look like their meaning, or like the things they name. Choose TEN words from your novel and try to write each word in a way that illustrates its meaning. Here are some examples:

- The word *smile* can be written as someone's smile in place of their teeth.
- The word *hairy* can be written with hairs all over it.
- The word *melt* can be written to look as though the letters are melting.

Picture Power

Each person in the group chooses ONE event from the novel you are all reading. Each of you writes the event on a small piece of paper to allow you to clearly remember what you have to describe when it is your turn. Do not let anybody else see what you have written. Each player then stands in front of the group and draws a picture to describe the event while the other people try to guess the exact event. The person who gets the event correct wins a point. Repeat until everyone has had a turn to play.

CARD 3

Character Silhouette

Silhouettes are human portraits in a solid black colour. They show the detailed outline of a person or figure, usually from the side angle. Draw an outline of a character from your novel. Cut out the silhouette with care so that the details are kept intact. Glue your silhouette onto a coloured scene from the novel and display it.

CARD 4

Character Cube

You will need a cube net for this activity. Choose ONE character from your novel as the basis for this activity. Write on each side of the cube so that it eventually describes the following about the character (you can also decorate your cube):

- Name
- Description
- Likes
- Dislikes
- Friends
- Goals.

Glorious Game

Create a board game based on your novel. Be creative and design your game using your own thoughts and ideas. Be sure your game:

- Is based on your novel

- Is suitable for two to four players

- Has clear instructions on how to play.

When you have put your game together, play it with other people in your group.

Storyline

1. Take an A3 piece of paper, turn the page landscape style, and then head it up with the name of the novel you are reading.

2. Now write the names of each of the main characters on the page, spreading the names out evenly down the left-hand side of the paper.

3. Draw a different line for each character.

4. Change the shape of the line to show changes to the character.

5. Think about what shape your line should be in order to show the important events experienced by this character.

6. When you have finished drawing your storylines for each character, label the lines at the major events or changes in order to explain what happened at these points.

Scene Selection

Choose a highly descriptive passage from your novel. Write this passage on the bottom of a piece of white paper. Draw a detailed picture to illustrate this description.

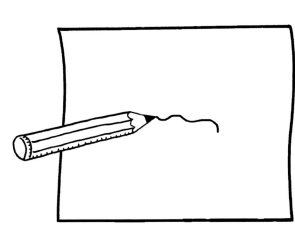

Character Composition

The author of the novel you are reading would like to introduce a new character. You have been asked to come up with this interesting new character.

1. Start by drawing a detailed picture of this character.

2. Write the character's name as the heading.

3. Label your drawing.

4. Write a brief description of the character underneath the illustration.

Mystical Mask

Create a character mask for ONE of the characters in your novel.
Each person in your group should create a mask based on a different
character. When the masks are complete,
everyone in the group places their mask
on their face and acts out a section of
the novel.

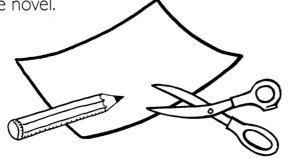

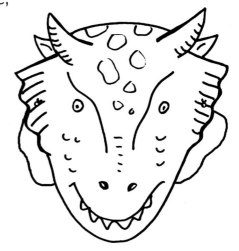

Unusual Expressions

Think about the many different emotions and reactions the characters
experienced throughout the novel. Choose FIVE of your favourite
character reactions from the novel. Draw a picture of each character's
facial expressions so as to portray this character's
different reactions. Label each face with the name
of the expression illustrated.

Magazine Cover

A popular teenage magazine, *Teen Read,* is doing a feature on your novel. They would like to put a picture from the novel on the front cover of their magazine.

1. Design the front cover of *Teen Read.*

2. Be sure to include the name of the magazine, the illustration from the novel, and a headline that relates to the illustration.

3. Make sure your illustration is eye-catching and your headline is short and appealing.

Driving Design

Imagine you are sitting in the back seat of a car. The car is moving slowly through the novel as you read. Look out of the window as the car moves along and draw a picture of the settings you observe as you drive through the story. Your picture should depict all the different locations in which the story takes place.

Novel Mobile

Think about the key characters, settings, objects and events that occurred in your novel. Draw a picture to represent these various aspects of the storyline. Hang them together with string to create a hanging storyline mobile.

Picturesque Place

Draw a picture of a place described in the novel. Be sure to include in your picture the details that are written in the novel. Create a close graphic representation of the author's description. Write a few sentences that describe your chosen setting from the novel.

Tissue Tales

Draw an outline of a shape described in the novel. This can be an object or a character. Collect pieces of tissue paper of different colours. Cut out the tissue paper to form the same shape. Place the tissue shapes in a random manner and glue them onto coloured paper. This artwork will create an attention-grabbing effect.

- -

Alternative Illustration

The author would like to reprint the novel you are reading but would like a different front cover. The author wants a new and improved cover that will appeal to children your age. Think carefully about the storyline when planning the cover. Be sure to consider colour, type font and illustrations in your design. Fold your new design around the novel to create a new book-cover jacket.

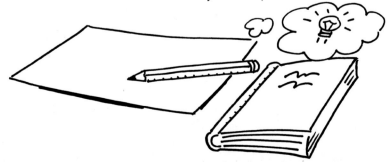

Graffiti Wall

Draw a brick wall across the whole page, and then write graffiti across the wall to represent the actions, phrases and events from the novel you are reading. Here are some examples: Dean was here; Rachel rocks; Georgia for School Representative Council; Matt loves Jane.

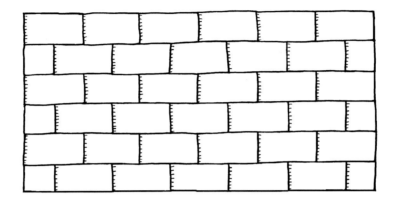

Cityscape Scene

Create a cityscape or landscape based on a place described in your novel. Start by turning your paper landscape style and drawing a line across the middle of the page. Now draw your cityscape or landscape so that the buildings or landforms rest on this line. Colour, label and display your cityscape or landscape.

Catalogue Portrait

You will need some grocery catalogues, scissors, paper and glue for this activity.

1. Choose **ONE** character from your novel as the basis of this activity.

2. Cut out pictures of fruit and vegetables.

3. Place these pictures together to create a portrait of your character that is made entirely out of fruit and vegetables.

4. Label your drawing and display it.

Terrific Topic

Choose a topic associated with the themes discussed within your novel. Write the topic as a heading on a piece of art paper and then create an artwork that links with your chosen topic. When you have finished your artwork, share it with your group and explain why you chose this particular topic.

Sequencing Story

Draw five separate pictures of key events in the storyline of the novel you are reading. Mix up the pictures and ask another person to arrange them in the same sequence as the events occurred in the novel.

Creative Capers

Different novels evoke different emotions and feelings in individuals. How does this novel make you feel? Express these positive and/or negative feelings by creating an abstract picture. Use bold colours and lines to show the depth of your feelings. Think carefully about the colours you choose to represent different emotions.

Reflecting and Responding

Aim

These activities require students to reflect on and respond to a particular aspect of the text. They require students to give a thoughtful, reflective response to the text. The activities enable students to respond in a personal manner to the text.

Interesting Development

When you read, have you ever thought about a similar event that you remember from another novel or film? When this happens, we are making connections and constructing comparisons between situations or similar events. Locate ONE incident from your novel and compare it with a similar event from another novel or film. Describe the connection between these events.

Great Game

Your group will need to work together on this activity. Create a board game based on your novel. Make the game board look like a map of the story. Have your counters represent characters in the story.

Write the procedure and rules needed to play the game. Finally, play the game together.

CARD 3

Character Talk

Imagine you could talk to one of the characters in your novel. What would you say? Draw a picture of yourself and the character in a scene from the novel. Insert speech bubbles to show the dialogue you exchange with this character.

CARD 4

Game Show

Your group will need to work together for this activity. Create a game show by first of all using the information and events from your novel to create a set of interesting question cards. Be sure to write the correct answer on the back of the card. When each player has written TEN question cards, choose someone in your group to shuffle the cards and put them together in a pile ready to start the game. You will need to decide who will be the host, the contestant, the friend on the phone offering the contestant advice, and the score-keeper.

Reaction Replay

You will need to work in groups of two or three for this activity. Choose an exciting or important event from the novel. Role play and act out this event. After you have practised your act, share it with the other members of your group.

Problematic Part

Pretend you are the author of the novel you are reading. Describe your experience as a writer developing this story. Describe the sections of the novel that were the most difficult to write and those that were the most fun to write.